# My Little Book of
# Volcanoes and
# Earthquakes

by Claudia Martin

Sandy Creek
NEW YORK

Sandy Creek
NEW YORK

An Imprint of Sterling Publishing
387 Park Avenue South
New York, NY 10016

Text © 2014 by QEB Publishing, Inc.
Illustrations © 2014 by QEB Publishing, Inc.

This 2014 edition published by Sandy Creek.

ISBN 978-1-4351-5531-2

Manufactured in Guangdong, China
Lot #:
2  4  6  8  10  9  7  5  3  1
04/14

Words in **bold** are
explained in the
glossary on page 60.

# Contents

# What is a volcano?

A **volcano** is a hole that goes down into the Earth. Sometimes melted rock, called **magma**, rushes up through the hole.

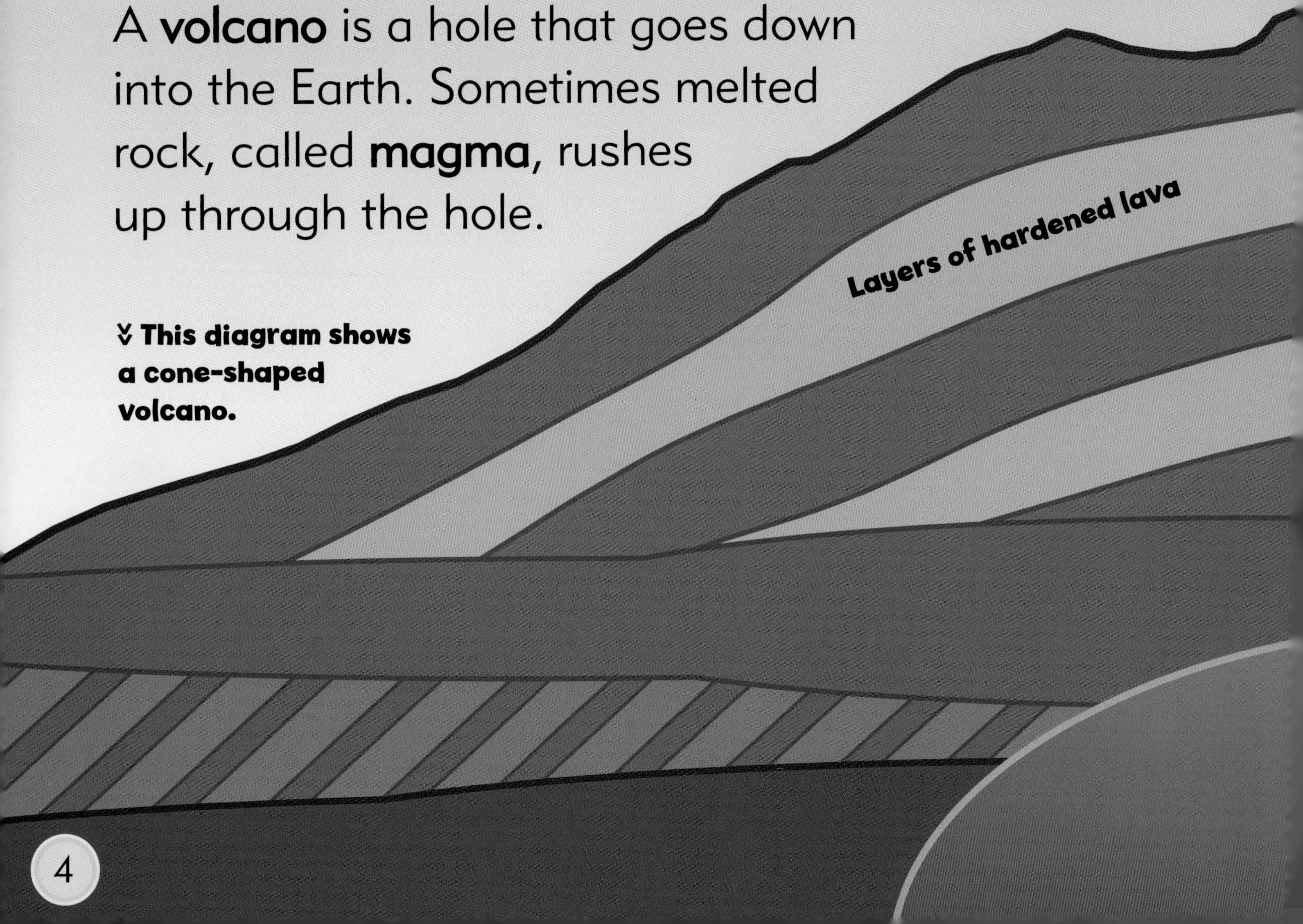

**⌄ This diagram shows a cone-shaped volcano.**

Layers of hardened lava

**Smoke and ash**

**Crater**

When magma reaches the surface we call it **lava**. Over time, layers of hardened lava can make a volcano high, like a mountain.

**Magma rises up**

Below the outer crust of the Earth is hot rock. In places, it gets so hot that it melts!

⌃ The bowl-shaped hole at the top of a volcano is called a crater.

# Eruption!

An **eruption** is when lava, gas and **ash** burst out of a volcano.

⌄ **Lava flows down the side of this volcano.**

There are different kinds of eruptions. Sometimes lava seeps out slowly. Sometimes it shoots out in a giant explosion, along with a cloud of ash and gas.

« **This volcano is belching out a cloud of ash and gas.**

>> **Some volcanoes have dramatic eruptions. Lava and sparks fly into the sky.**

# Lava

When melted rock reaches the surface, we call it lava. Burning-hot lava destroys everything in its way.

« This house has been buried in lava. Luckily, the people who lived here escaped in time.

Thin, runny lava can flow downhill at more than 70 miles an hour —much faster than a person can run! Thick lava moves more slowly.

« This thick lava is oozing slowly downhill.

⌃ When lava cools, it hardens into solid rock. This rocky landscape was made by lava flows.

# Ash

Some eruptions are so violent that they blast melted rock into billions of pieces—from big lumps to powdery ash and dust.

<< This home in Java has been covered in ash and dust by an eruption.

« Ash clouds can stay in the sky for weeks. They make it dangerous for airplanes to fly.

In the deadliest eruptions, there is no lava at all. Ash, hot gas and rocks race down the mountain. This is called a **pyroclastic flow**.

^ Pyroclastic flows can move faster than an airplane.

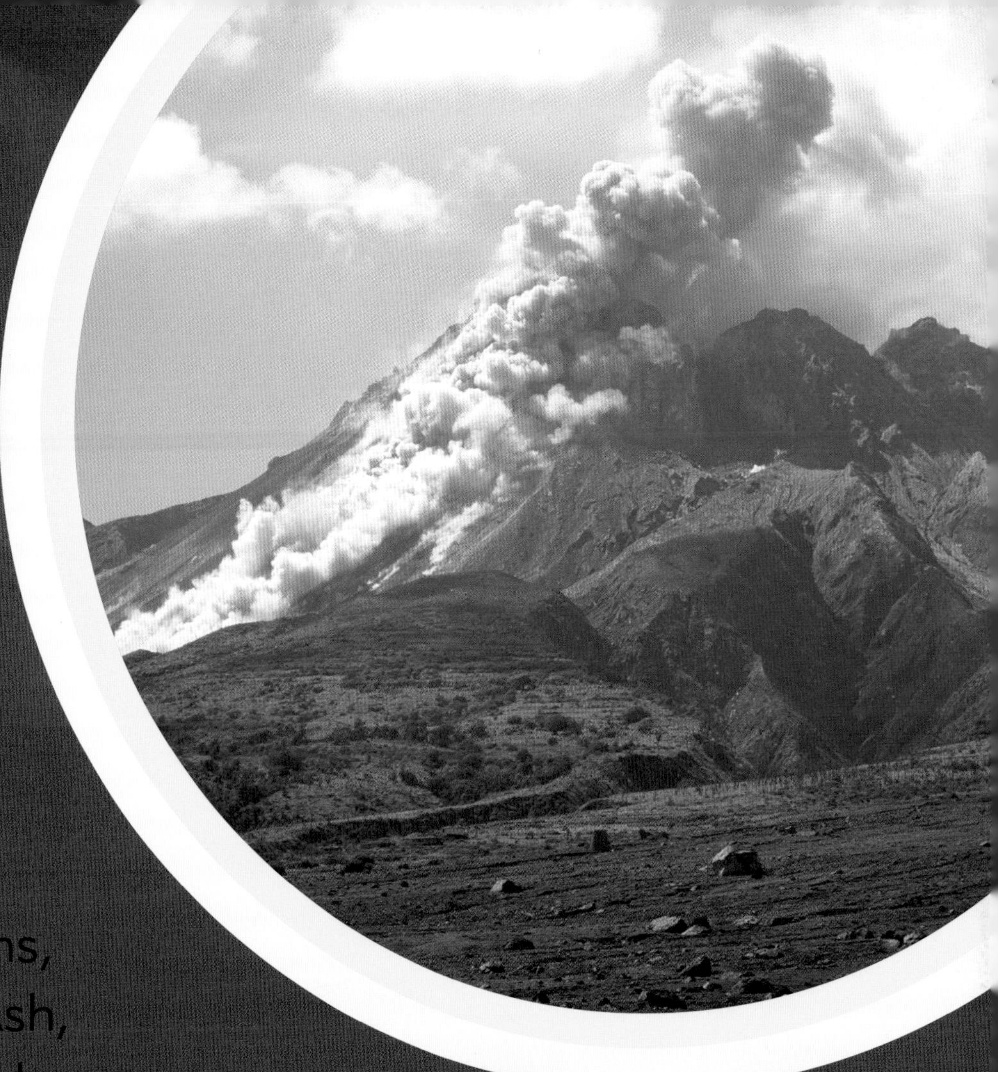

# Volcano shapes

Every time a volcano erupts, a new layer of lava is left to harden around it. This often builds up to make a cone shape.

« Shield volcanoes are less pointy than cone-shaped volcanoes.

Not all volcanoes are cone-shaped. **Shield volcanoes** are the shape of a warrior's shield. Lava can also pour out of a crack in the ground known as a fissure vent.

» **This huge crack in the ground is a fissure vent. During an eruption, lava pours out of the crack.**

# Supervolcanoes

**Supervolcanoes** are the largest volcanoes of all. Their eruptions are thousands of times larger than an ordinary volcano's.

⌄ **The eruption of a supervolcano often leaves a massive hole called a** caldera. **This one has filled with water.**

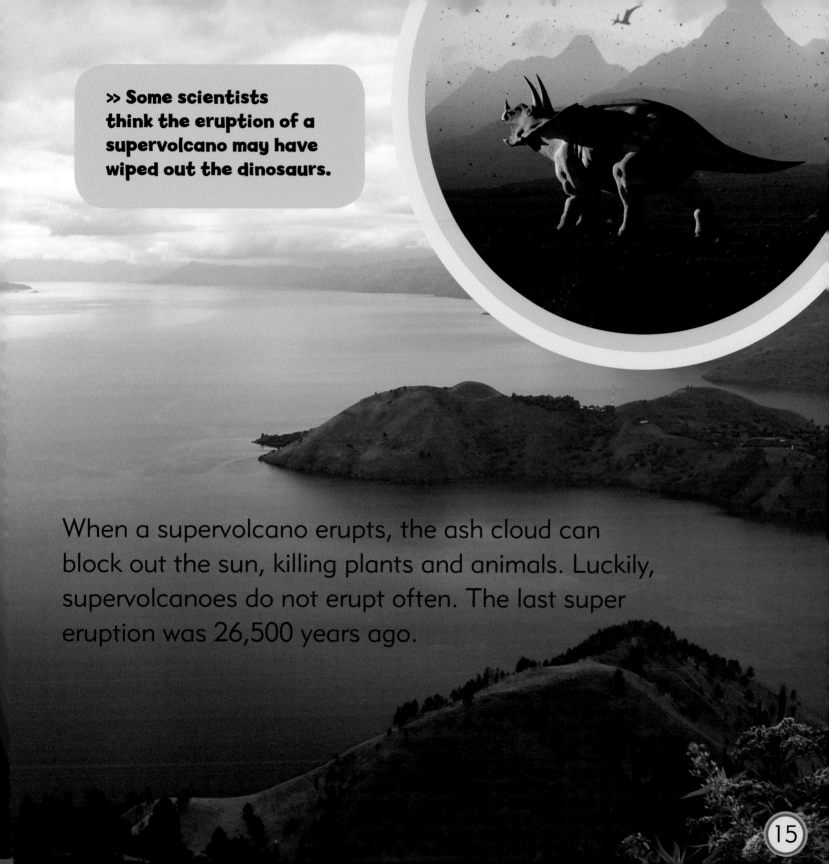

>> Some scientists think the eruption of a supervolcano may have wiped out the dinosaurs.

When a supervolcano erupts, the ash cloud can block out the sun, killing plants and animals. Luckily, supervolcanoes do not erupt often. The last super eruption was 26,500 years ago.

# Geysers

A **geyser** is a fountain of water that is heated by boiling rocks beneath the Earth.

>> **This geyser in Iceland shoots water up to 130 feet high.**

In some places close to volcanoes, water below the ground gets very hot. It bursts up through a crack in the Earth with a spray of hot water and steam.

>> This bubbling mud has also been heated by magma. It is called a mud pot.

# Active or extinct?

A volcano that could erupt is called an **active volcano**. But some volcanoes are old and will not erupt again—they are **extinct**.

>> Edinburgh Castle in Scotland is built on an extinct volcano.

A **dormant volcano** is one that has not erupted for thousands of years—but might erupt again. Sometimes it is hard to tell if a volcano is extinct or dormant.

⌃ This is the crater of a dormant volcano in Hawaii. Perhaps one day it will erupt again.

⌃ Mount Rainier in Washington looks peaceful, but it is a very dangerous active volcano.

# Where are volcanoes?

>> Mt. Vesuvius in Italy is near the edge of a plate.

Earth's crust is not in one piece: it is in parts, called **plates**.

>> This map shows the plates that make up Earth's crust.

**North America**

**South America**

### Map Key

 **Major volcano**

 **Other volcanoes**

 **Plates**

⌃ This line of volcanoes in Guatemala, Central America, is near the edge of a plate.

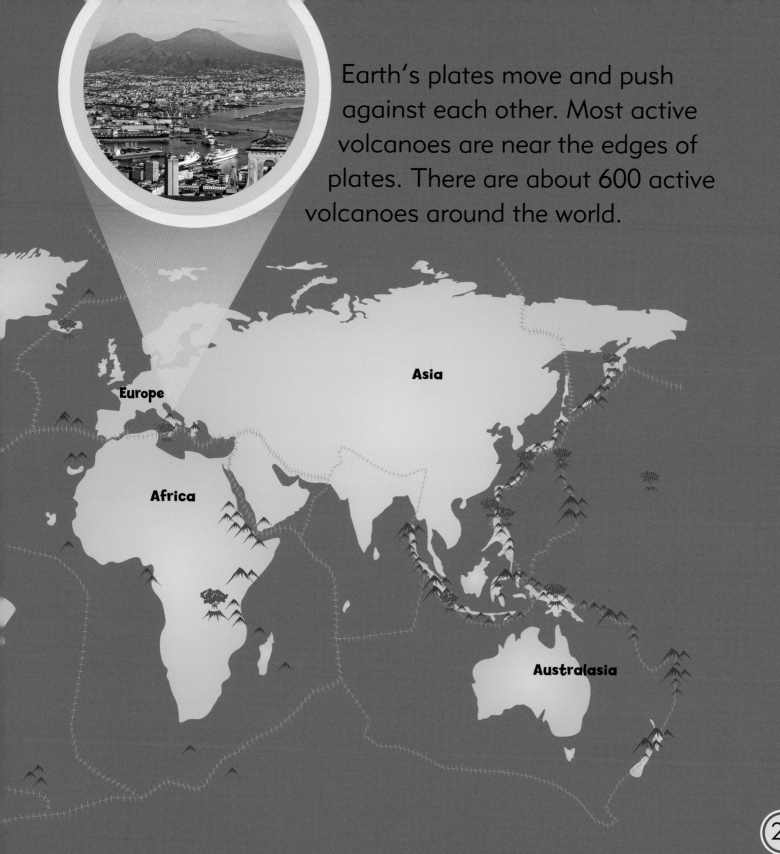

Earth's plates move and push against each other. Most active volcanoes are near the edges of plates. There are about 600 active volcanoes around the world.

Europe

Asia

Africa

Australasia

# Studying volcanoes

People who study volcanoes are called **volcanologists**. They do very important work that saves lives.

˅ Volcanologists have to be careful near hot lava.

« Volcanologists wear heat-proof clothing to take lava samples.

Volcanologists look for signs that a volcano is about to erupt. They measure the volcano to see if it is swelling with magma. They check if the ground is getting hotter.

>> Many volcanoes are safe to visit even if you're not a volcanologist.

23

# Living near a volcano

Millions of people live close to active volcanoes. When their volcano erupts, they have to move out of the way—fast!

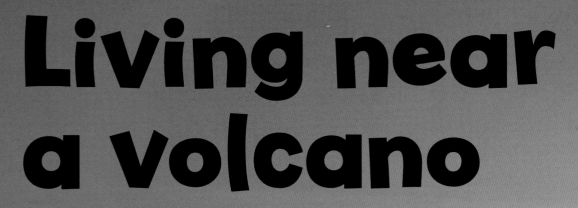

« People wear masks to protect themselves from ash.

If you are near a volcano that starts erupting, you may be told to leave the area. Make sure you follow instructions—and don't panic.

« 12 million people live near Mount Fuji in Japan.

# Useful Volcanoes

⌄ Mount Etna in Italy is an active volcano. Its slopes are covered by farms.

Volcanoes can be useful. That is often why people choose to live on their slopes.

« Bananas need warmth to grow. In Iceland, heat from underground is used to warm greenhouses.

The ash that volcanoes spew out makes the soil perfect for farming. The heat around volcanoes can be used to warm homes and make electricity.

>> **Heat from magma in Iceland warms this pool and makes electricity in a power station.**

# St. Helens

Mount St. Helens is an active volcano in Washington. Volcanologists say it could erupt at any time.

In May 1980, a huge earthquake caused Mount St. Helens to erupt. An explosion of rock, gas, and ash flattened buildings and killed 57 people.

>> The 1980 eruption lasted for nine hours. It left the volcano 1,300 feet shorter.

∧ The crater of Mount St. Helens is full of ice and snow.

# Vesuvius

Mount Vesuvius in Italy is one of the world's most dangerous volcanoes. Around three million people live nearby.

⌄ **Today you can visit the ruins of Pompeii or look inside the crater of Mount Vesuvius.**

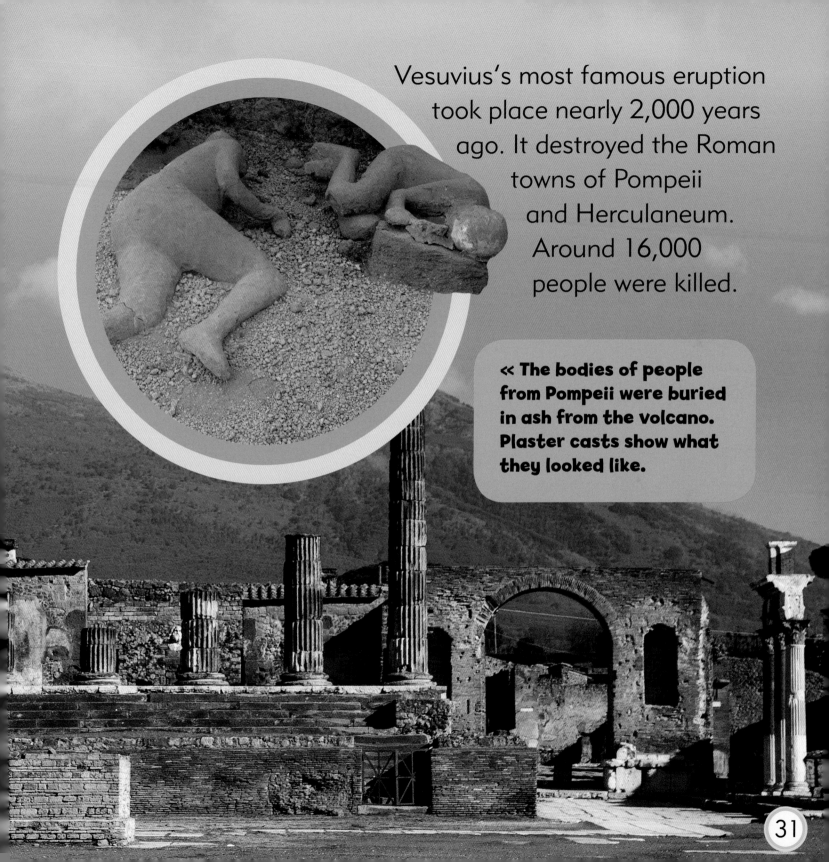

Vesuvius's most famous eruption took place nearly 2,000 years ago. It destroyed the Roman towns of Pompeii and Herculaneum. Around 16,000 people were killed.

« The bodies of people from Pompeii were buried in ash from the volcano. Plaster casts show what they looked like.

# Mauna Kea

Measured from its base on the sea floor, Mauna Kea is the highest mountain on the planet. It is 33,130 feet tall.

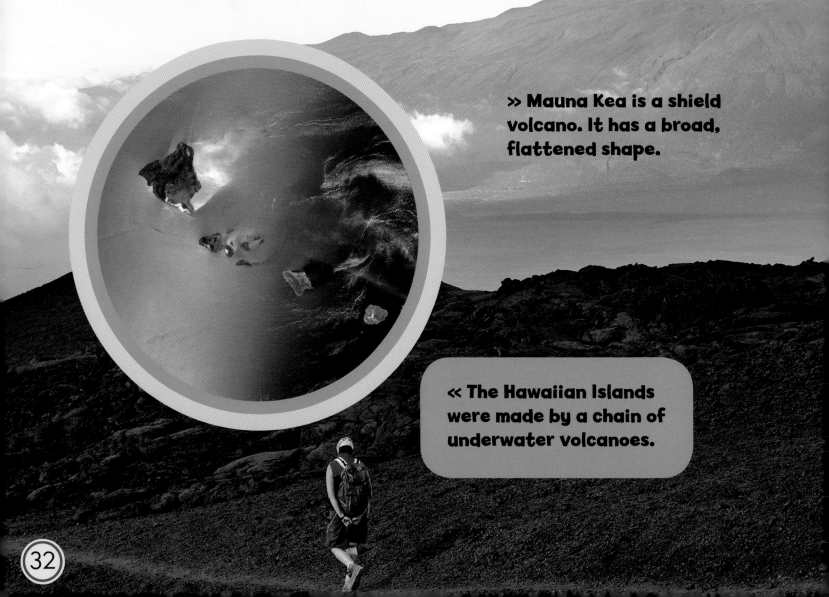

>> Mauna Kea is a shield volcano. It has a broad, flattened shape.

<< The Hawaiian Islands were made by a chain of underwater volcanoes.

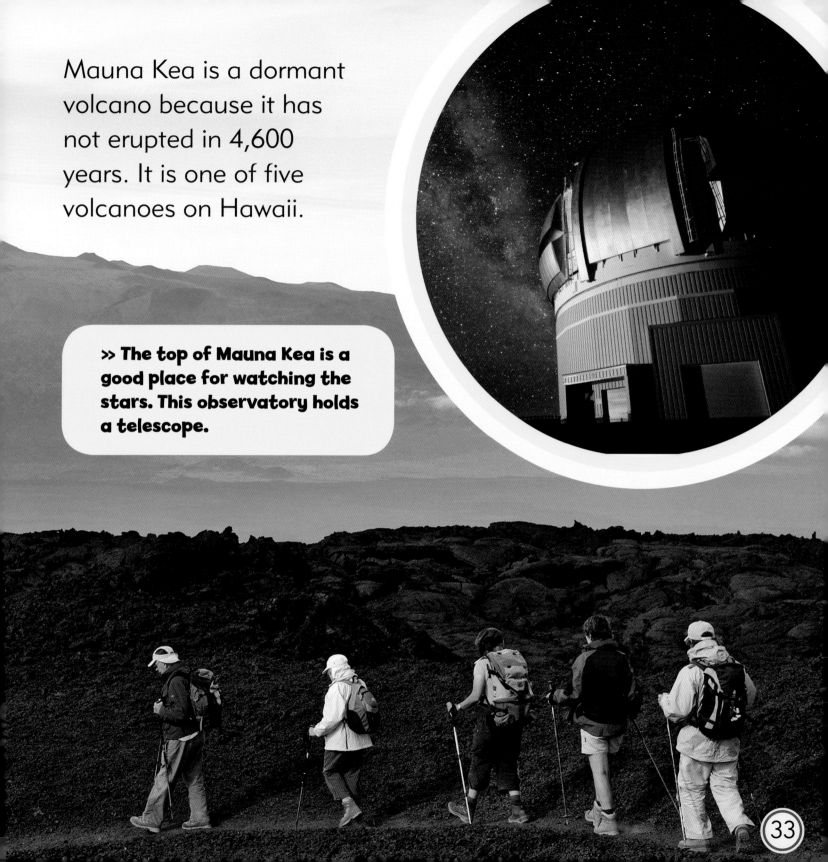

Mauna Kea is a dormant volcano because it has not erupted in 4,600 years. It is one of five volcanoes on Hawaii.

>> The top of Mauna Kea is a good place for watching the stars. This observatory holds a telescope.

# Krakatoa

Krakatoa was a small volcanic island in Indonesia. When the volcano erupted in 1883, it made one of the loudest sounds ever heard.

⌃ **Anak Krakatau has replaced Krakatoa. It grows by 16 feet every year.**

The eruption destroyed most of the island of Krakatoa. Later eruptions built a new island in the same spot. It is called Anak Krakatau, which means "Child of Krakatoa."

>> Anak Krakatau hurls out lava.

# Volcanoes under the sea

Most of the world's volcanoes are not on land. They are under the seas and oceans.

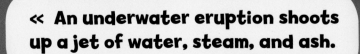
<< An underwater eruption shoots up a jet of water, steam, and ash.

✓ **White Island, off the coast of New Zealand, is the top of an underwater volcano.**

⌃ **This diver is taking the temperature of an underwater volcano.**

When an underwater volcano erupts, lava pours from a hole in the sea floor. The lava hardens and starts to build a cone. The tallest cones rise above the water and make islands.

# Volcanoes in space

Earth is not the only planet in our Solar System with volcanoes. Photos taken by spacecraft show volcanoes on other planets and moons.

« Jupiter's moon Io is dotted with volcanoes.

The largest volcano in the Solar System is Olympus Mons on Mars. It is 80,000 feet high—more than twice the size of Mauna Kea, the tallest mountain on Earth.

⌄ **Olympus Mons has not erupted in the last 2 million years.**

>> **Maat Mons is the tallest volcano on Venus. There are more than 1,600 volcanoes on the planet.**

# What is an earthquake?

An earthquake is when the surface of the Earth moves. The ground shakes and cracks open.

**>> During a large earthquake, the ground's shaking can knock down buildings.**

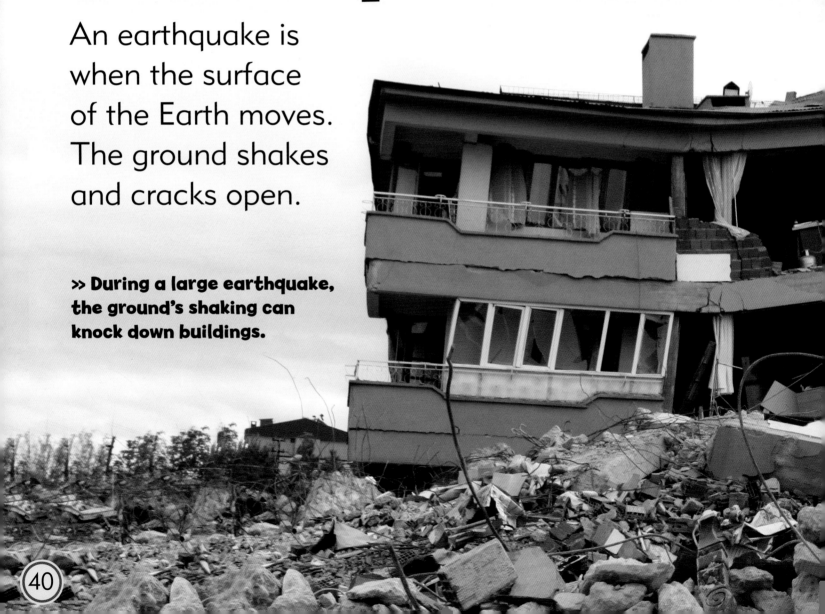

There are about 500,000 earthquakes every year. Most of them are too small to be felt, but the strongest earthquakes are terrifying.

⋀ Earthquakes can make big cracks appear in the ground.

# Why the earth moves

Earth is wrapped in a layer of hard rock called the crust. The crust is in huge pieces called plates.

**>> This map shows the plates that lie beneath the ground. The red dots are the sites of big earthquakes.**

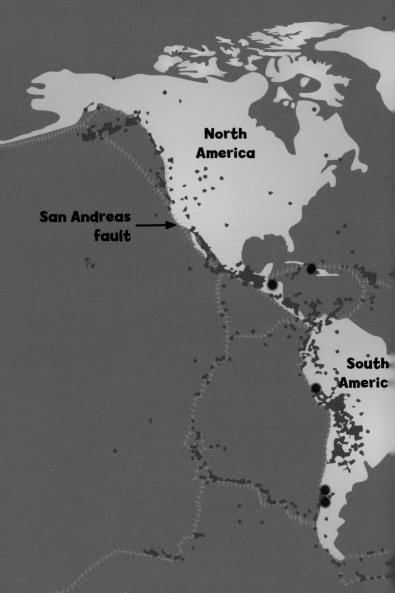

North America

San Andreas fault

South Americ

**Map Key**

⬤ Deadliest earthquakes

⬤ Other earthquakes

⟋⟋⟋⟋⟋⟋ Plates

The plates move very, very slowly. Sometimes plates stick as they slide past each other. They judder and shake. This causes an earthquake.

Europe

Asia

Africa

Australasia

⌃ The places where plates meet are called faults. Some can be seen above ground. This is the San Andreas fault in California.

# Shockwaves

The place where an earthquake starts is called its **epicenter**. An earthquake spreads out from its epicenter in **shockwaves**.

<< Shockwaves race out from the epicenter of an earthquake.

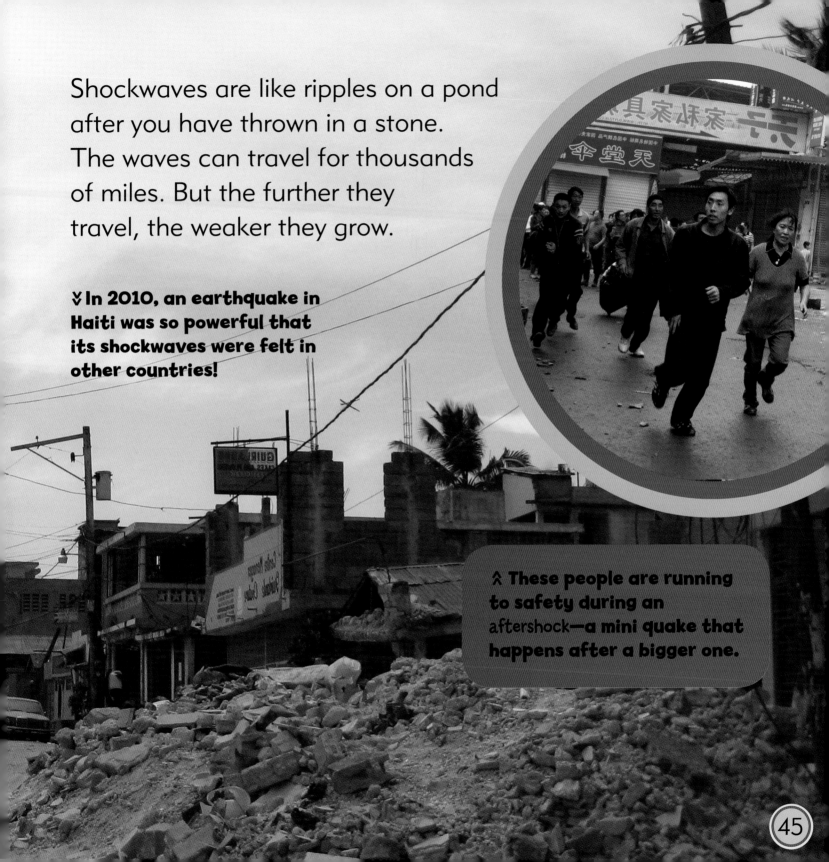

Shockwaves are like ripples on a pond after you have thrown in a stone. The waves can travel for thousands of miles. But the further they travel, the weaker they grow.

▿ In 2010, an earthquake in Haiti was so powerful that its shockwaves were felt in other countries!

⌃ These people are running to safety during an aftershock—a mini quake that happens after a bigger one.

# Earthquake damage

A fierce earthquake can make buildings crack, bend, or fall down. People may be hurt or trapped beneath the rubble.

⌄ Strong metal bars are used to support buildings after an earthquake.

« If an earthquake damages gas pipes or electricity lines, fires may break out.

Toppling buildings are not the only danger in a big earthquake. Floods and fires caused by earthquakes can also do terrible damage.

⌄ **Earthquakes can make bridges and roads collapse.**

# Landslides

Landslides, mudslides, and **avalanches** can all be set off by an earthquake.

⌄ **The people who lived in this house had to get out quickly!**

When the Earth shakes, it can loosen rocks, mud, and snow in the mountains. When they slide down onto homes, things can get scary!

>> In an avalanche, snow rushes downhill at more than 180 miles an hour.

# Tsunamis

If an earthquake happens under the sea, it can make giant waves called **tsunamis**.

When a tsunami reaches land, the wall of water can wash away everything in its path. If you are by the sea during an earthquake, head for high ground straight away.

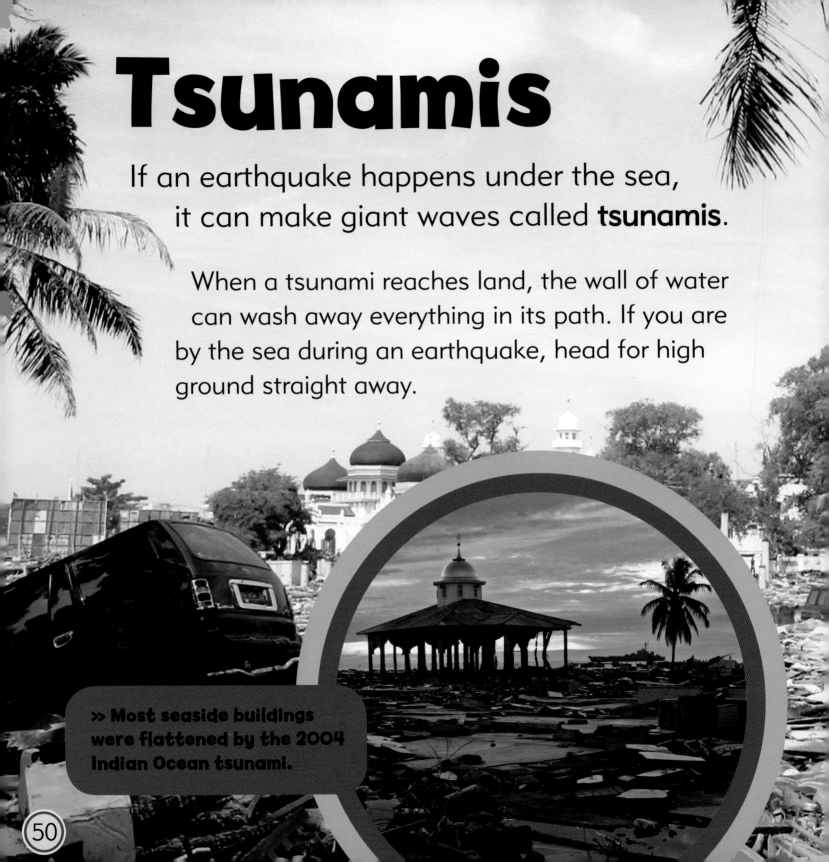

>> **Most seaside buildings were flattened by the 2004 Indian Ocean tsunami.**

▽ A tsunami hit the coast of Thailand in 2004. It was started by an earthquake under the Indian Ocean.

# Studying earthquakes

People who study earthquakes are called **seismologists**. They warn everyone if an earthquake could be on the way.

Seismologists use machines called **seismometers** to measure earthquakes. Each earthquake is given a number that tells us how strong it is.

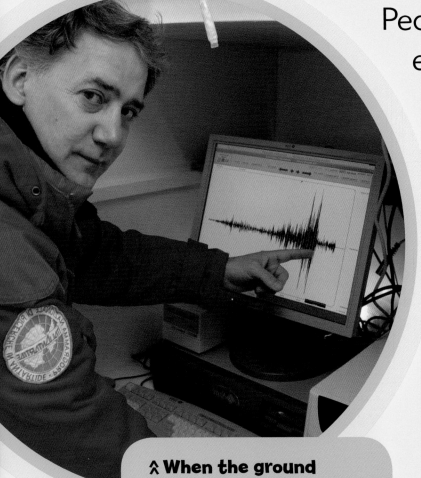

⌃ **When the ground shakes the seismometer draws a wiggly line.**

8    Whole cities
     are destroyed.

7    Ground cracks.
     Whole buildings fall down.

6    Walls fall down.

5    Furniture moves around.
     Buildings are damaged.

4    Felt by lots of people.
     Walls crack.

3    Feels like a truck
     going past.

2    Usually cannot
     be felt by people.

1    Cannot be felt by people.

# Strong buildings

The greatest danger in an earthquake is toppling buildings. Today we can make buildings that do not fall when the ground shakes.

>> **The Transamerica Pyramid in San Francisco, has special supports. It survived a big earthquake in 1989.**

Buildings can be made so that they bend and sway with Earth's movements without breaking.

Unfortunately, earthquakes often happen in poorer countries where many people cannot afford to build strong homes.

⌃ The Gakuen Cocoon Tower in Tokyo, Japan, was built to survive even the worst earthquakes.

# To the rescue

As soon as the shaking stops, rescuers rush to help. They find people who are trapped inside buildings or underneath rubble.

« Rescue dogs sniff out people who are hidden under the rubble.

Rescuers put out fires and clear away rubble. Then they help people find shelter and food while their homes are rebuilt.

⌄ Rescue teams are trained to find people after an earthquake.

⌃ Food is delivered to people who have lost their homes.

# Earthquake safety

Do you know what to do if you are in an earthquake? There are lots of ways you and your family can stay safe.

⩔ **If you are outside, move away from buildings and protect your head.**

In places that often have earthquakes, people practice what to do if one happens. Being prepared means that fewer people will be hurt.

**« If you are indoors, take cover under a strong table.**

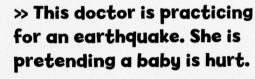

**» This doctor is practicing for an earthquake. She is pretending a baby is hurt.**

# Glossary

**active volcano**  A volcano that could erupt at any time.

**aftershock**  Smaller shakes of the ground that follow an earthquake.

**ash**  Little dust-like pieces of lava made by an exploding volcano.

**avalanche**  A sudden slide of snow down a mountainside.

**caldera**  A huge hollow in the ground. It is made by a volcano caving in after an eruption.

**crater**  A bowl-shaped hole at the top of a volcano.

**crust**  The hard outer layer of Earth.

**dormant volcano**  A volcano that has not erupted for a very long time but could erupt again.

**earthquake**  Shaking of the ground. An earthquake is caused by movements of Earth's plates.

**epicenter**  The point on Earth's surface where an earthquake starts.

**eruption**  When a volcano sends out bursts of lava, gas, or ash.

**extinct volcano**  A volcano that will never erupt again. An extinct volcano no longer has a supply of magma.

**fault** A place where Earth's plates touch and rub against each other. Volcanoes and earthquakes are often on faults.

**gas** A substance that is not solid or runny. The air is made of gases.

**geyser** An opening in the ground that lets out jets of hot water and steam.

**lava** Hot, melted rock that comes out of a volcano.

**magma** Hot, melted rock inside the Earth.

**plate** A giant piece of the Earth's crust.

**pyroclastic flow** A burning cloud of rocks, ash, and gas made by an erupting volcano.

**seismologist** A person who studies earthquakes.

**seismometer** A machine for measuring the Earth's shaking during an earthquake.

**shield volcano** A volcano that is shaped like a warrior's shield lying flat on the ground.

**shockwaves** Movements that travel through the ground from the center of an earthquake.

**supervolcano** A very large volcano. A supervolcano's eruptions are thousands of times bigger than an ordinary volcano's.

**tsunami** A giant ocean wave.

**volcano** A hole in the Earth's crust where lava can escape.

**volcanologist** A person who studies volcanoes.

# Index

# Picture credits

(t=top, b=bottom, l=left, r=right, c=center, fc=front cover, bc=back cover)

**CORBIS**
bcr Lloyd Cluff, 13c James Hardy/PhotoAlto, 22–23, 22l Roger Ressmeyer, 24bl, 64 YT HARYONO/Reuters, 26l, 27r Bob Krist, 29tr Ocean, 36l LOTHAR SLABON/epa, 39r NASA/Corbis, 38l NASA/JPL/USGS/Michael Benson/Kinetikon Pictures, 38–39 NASA/Roger Ressmeyer, 43r Lloyd Cluff, 45 Elisa Haberer, 49r Menno Boermans/Aurora Photos, 50l James Robert Fuller, 58–59b ROMEO RANOCO/Reuters, 59br NIR ELIAS/Reuters, 58–59t ISSEI KATO/Reuters

**Dreamstime**
8l Fransen, 44–45 FabioConcetta, 47 Martyn Unsworth

**Getty Images**
bcbl Art Wolfe, 10–11 Ulla Lohmann, 16–17 Martin Child, 30–31 Cultura Travel/Lost Horizon Images, 32–33 Sami Sarkis, 33tr Philip Rosenberg, 34–35 De Agostini / C. Dani & I. Jeske, 35 Philippe Crochet, 36–37 David Wall Photo, 46–47 Bruce Hands, 48–49 Getty Images, 50–51 Getty Images

**NASA**
32c Jacques Descloitres, MODIS Land Rapid Response Team

**Shutterstock** fc beboy, bctl George W. Bailey, bcc Cico, bcbr Siim Sepp ,1, 6–7  beboy, 2–3 wdeon, 4–5 George W. Bailey, 5r cesc_assawin, 7tl Warren Goldswain, 7br Rainer Albiez, 8–9 Vadim Petrakov, 9t Siim Sepp, 10l Brisbane, 12–13 robert cicchetti, 12l DmitrySerbin, 14–15 Hendrik H, 17r Karin Wassmer, 18c godrick, 18–19 Jeff Zenner Photography, 19t Lisa Hoang, 20–21, 42–43 Designua, 20c cleanfotos, 21tl Zyankarlo, 23r Tappasan Phurisamrit, 24–25 skyearth, 26–27 ollirg, 28–29 Valeriy Poltorak, 31t Alessandro Colle, 40–41 fpolat69, 41r Naypong, 46 vikau, 54–55 Rudy Mareel, 55r Sean Pavone, 56–57 Prometheus72, 56–57 fotostory, 57r Lakeview Images

**Science Photo Library**
11r BERNHARD EDMAIER, 15 MARK GARLICK, 37t ALEXIS ROSENFELD, 52 KARIM AGABI/EURELIOS